ROBOTICS™

HOW TO BUILD A
PRIZE-WINNING
ROBOT

JOEL CHAFFEE

rosen publishing's
rosen
central®

NEW YORK

Published in 2011 by The Rosen Publishing Group, Inc.
29 East 21st Street, New York, NY 10010

Copyright © 2011 by The Rosen Publishing Group, Inc.

First Edition

Library of Congress Cataloging-in-Publication Data

Chaffee, Joel.
How to build a prize-winning robot / Joel Chaffee. — 1st ed.
    p. cm. — (Robotics)
Includes bibliographical references and index.
ISBN 978-1-4488-1238-7 (library binding)
ISBN 978-1-4488-2252-2 (pbk.)
ISBN 978-1-4488-2255-3 (6-pack)
1. Robots–Design and construction–Juvenile literature. 2. Robots–Design
and construction–Competitions–United States–Juvenile literature. 3.
Robotics–Juvenile literature. I. Title.
TJ211.2.C53 2011
629.8'92079–dc22

                                                          2010025748

Manufactured in the United States of America

CPSIA Compliance Information: Batch #W11YA: For further information, contact Rosen Publishing, New York, New York,
at 1-800-237-9932.

On the cover: A soccer robot competes during the RoboCup robotics
competition.

CONTENTS

INTRODUCTION

Robotics competitions have in recent years sprung about all over the United States and worldwide. They are predominantly called "robotics competitions" and involve robots competing against one another, performing designated tasks to win a prize. But that is just about all they have in common. Beyond this, they differ in focus, size, prize money, qualification criteria, and about a dozen other parameters. One needs to

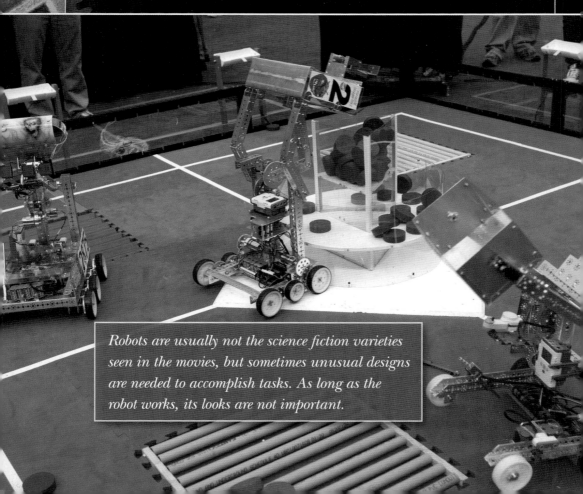

Robots are usually not the science fiction varieties seen in the movies, but sometimes unusual designs are needed to accomplish tasks. As long as the robot works, its looks are not important.

keep all of this in mind when choosing a competition to enter—a competition into which a serious competitor will invest great time and effort.

The most important thing to realize about robotics competitions is that winning a competition is more than just building a robot. The skills involved go beyond engineering and science; teamwork, management skills, good communication, discipline, and the ability to do detailed testing and learn from mistakes are also required. Being a genius like Albert Einstein or Thomas Edison won't guarantee success. Also, not being the greatest robot builder in the world is no reason to despair. Competitions are won by simple ideas that work, not by ingenious contraptions that never get off the ground. However, on the playing field a team could have the best robot, but without the proper strategy, they will not win.

CHAPTER 1
Picking Your Competition

obotics research is closely related to work done at universities and some government agencies, so entry into robotics competitions is sometimes restricted to such institutions. In particular, many competitions are limited to student teams. Some are less restrictive than others, and sometimes it is enough to have a single student on the team. In other instances, however, not only do all members of the team need to be students, but they must all be either high school students or undergrads or some other particular specification. This restriction is, for example, imposed by the competition held annually by the Marine Academy of Technology and Environmental Science (MATES). Other restrictions of this type can exist, and you should look into them to be sure your team would be eligible to compete in the first place.

COMPETITION BASICS

The competition needs to be far enough in advance for proper preparation of the robot. This usually takes a much longer time than initially planned, which must be kept in mind for planners. Think about how much time can realistically be allocated to the goal. When in doubt, be conservative about the estimate, and if it seems there will not be enough time to prepare, there probably won't be. Competition winners choose competitions that allow time for building and testing.

If you are in the competition to win it (and who isn't?), then it is a good idea to examine what the winnings are. Is there a prize, and what is it? Sometimes the prize is cash that you may spend however you like. At other times the prize is something else, like a scholarship, a job, a piece of equipment, or money toward a future project. Sometimes it is a combination of the two; but it can also simply be prestige in the robot-building community, and there may be no actual material prize.

How much money can be spent on the project is very important, and it will determine how competitive the project can realistically be. You may be a serious enthusiast and willing to back knowledge and expertise with a reasonable sum of money from private or family sources. But for some types of competitions, your personal resources simply won't have a chance against those backed by a large institutional sponsor, such as a university. If you are looking to win the DARPA challenge (currently consisting of building a vehicle capable of navigating an urban environment) and grabbing the $2 million prize, it will require facing teams from Stanford, MIT, and the like, with nearly limitless budgets. And some components, such as sensors, microcontrollers, and such, simply cost money and cannot be improvised upon.

ROBOTICS COMPETITIONS, CAREER ACADEMIES, AND UNDERWATER ROBOTICS EDUCATION

Underwater robotics competitions are extremely popular, like the ROV (Remotely Operated Underwater Vehicle) challenge, sponsored by the Marine Academy of Technology and Environmental Science (MATES).

THE MARINE ACADEMY OF TECHNOLOGY AND ENVIRONMENTAL SCIENCE (MATES) IS A HIGH SCHOOL ACADEMY FOR STUDENTS WHO EXCEL IN SCIENCE AND MATHEMATICS. LOCATED IN NEW JERSEY, MATES HAS BEEN OPEN SINCE 2001, DRAWING STUDENTS FROM THE OCEAN COUNTY PUBLIC SCHOOL SYSTEM. OTHER CAREER ACADEMIES LIKE MATES ARE POPPING UP AROUND THE COUNTRY, SUCH AS THE MARINE ADVANCED TECHNOLOGY EDUCATION CENTER (MATE) IN MONTEREY, CA. OTHERS, LIKE MOUNTAIN HOME HIGH SCHOOL IN ARIZONA AND FLOYD COUNTY SCHOOLS COLLEGE AND CAREER ACADEMY, FEATURE ROBOTICS TEAMS.

Realizing this early on and focusing effort on competitions that can realistically be won, given the budget, is a very smart decision to make, saving plenty of frustration and disappointment later on.

TYPES OF COMPETITIONS

Competitions vary in many ways. They can be indoor or outdoor, which often makes a lot of difference because outdoor competitions could involve the natural elements, such as wind and rain. They can even take place in a completely different medium, such as in the air or underwater. Obviously all this drastically affects the design of your robot.

In some competitions robots are supposed to be entirely unmanned

RoboCup is aimed at promoting artificial intelligence and creative designs. The competition hopes its innovations will be useful in developing robotic emergency personnel.

("autonomous"), while in others one can keep control over them via remote control ("teleoperated"). There can also be a combination of the two. Typically robots start out on their own for a designated number of seconds, and once that period expires users can control them.

The central matter of what a competition is about is of course the nature of the task the robot is expected to do. This is the single most important factor that fundamentally affects the design. Sometimes the focus can be on locomotion, speed, and path-finding skills, such as in the previously mentioned DARPA competition. In other competitions it can be more about swimming and hovering. Others focus on manipulations, and the objective relates more to precision than speed and locomotion. In this case the design of the arm/grabbing device is crucial.

Apart from the two major categories described above, there are many other types of competitions, some quite funny and sometimes bizarre. For instance, RoboCup pits robots against one another in a soccer-playing competition. RoboGames involves a variety of challenges, mimicking the human Olympics, with wrestling, jumping, and other tasks. More exotic competitions are emerging by the day.

DO YOUR RESEARCH

Once the choices are narrowed down to a few candidates, it is time to look deeper into competition history. Look at the competitions that attracted attention, and examine past winners and competitors. Is the competition established and will it be around this year? What did some of the previous designs consist of? What did the robots do? Is this something that can be matched or bettered? Would accomplishing this be within budget constraints and expertise level?

Finally you must determine if you have the drive to win that competition. Is it exciting? Is it worth months, maybe more, working in a team, spending hour after hour building the robot, testing it, going through painstaking building and testing cycles, solving problem after problem, just for the competition and a chance to win it? If so, the next step is creating a solid team.

CHAPTER 2
Forming Your Team

The first step in forming a team to build your competition robot is finding a mentor. A mentor is someone who has enormous experience in the field and is willing to help the team a little bit along the way. Ideally, the mentor should be as excited about the project as the team is and really pulling for success.

In a school, the mentor will typically be a teacher, professor, or some other staff member who will have the expertise and the authority to have his or her advice considered and accepted. It is best if the mentor has had some direct experience not only with building robots, but also with attending, and ideally winning, robot competitions. The role of the mentor is most important when things are not running smoothly and problems are encountered.

CHOOSING TEAM MEMBERS

Sometimes teammates will be selected by the competitors, sometimes by someone else. Whatever the case, it is important to understand from the beginning that what makes a great team is a group of people who have diverse skills. In practice, this means people who are not alike and have skills the others lack.

Obviously, all team members need to share the same dedication, discipline, and desire to achieve the goal, but covering some specific abilities will greatly increase the speed with which problems are solved, new ideas are illuminated, and the team is able to move forward. Some of these are:

Communication is the most important aspect of being part of a robotics team. Students will often learn more in a brief conversation with a teammate than in hours of reading.

Experience with robot competitions and building robots in general: If someone on the team has been through the process before, his or her experience will be very valuable, especially if the mentor won't be able to provide it.

Leadership: The ability to assume responsibility and lead the team forward, maintain discipline, and adhere to the schedule.

Engineering skills: Understanding of the underlying science. Engineering skills are the essential part of a robot-building team and include having the grasp of "hard" science, solving problems creatively, being able to draw up designs, knowing how to judge component requirements, assessing the feasibility of construction, and many others.

Practical skills: Working with different materials and components, construction skills (soldering, welding, etc.).

Programming: Experience in programming the microcontroller and general proficiency in the programming languages used.

Graphic design skills: Some groups, such as USFIRST, work with community outreach. A member with graphic design skills would be able to design material to hand out at competitions.

Optimal team size will vary depending on the competition, but as a rule of thumb anywhere between three and ten members is a good number. This allows for enough diversity without complicated management. A team of a dozen or more members slowly becomes a serious organization. A stricter division of labor is appropriate and strong specializations become more common.

Robotics competitions, including USFIRST, are available for all age groups. Competing is one of the best ways to become involved in the field.

FINDING YOUR TOOLS

ACCESS TO EQUIPMENT, MATERIALS, AND SPACE IS NOT A SKILL, EXACTLY, BUT IS DEFINITELY IMPORTANT FOR COMPETITION PLANNING. SOME COMPONENTS CAN BE HARD TO FIND, SO BEING ABLE TO READILY ACQUIRE THEM SAVES A LOT OF TIME AND TROUBLE. ACCESS TO CONVENIENT SPACE FOR ASSEMBLY AND PROPER TESTING IS ALSO IMPORTANT AND SHOULD NOT BE UNDERESTIMATED.

SCHEDULING

The timeline for the project will depend on when the competition is and how much time can be given per week to work on it. That is understandable. What is often surprising to newcomers is how often and how quickly one can fall behind schedule. There are many potential roadblocks—a necessary component is three weeks late, a team member goes on a vacation or drops out, programming the robot to do that "simple" function takes three weeks instead of two hours. If some of these happen and are not planned and accounted for, you'll find yourself in a situation all too familiar to competition teams. In these situations one or more of the following usually happens: more and more time is allocated to the project and other aspects of life suffer as a consequence; the team does last-minute "hacking," hoping things will miraculously work; or the team drops functionalities and focuses on what can be done in the time remaining. Or the team just gives up.

One may avoid this by listening to the old saying of Benjamin Franklin: "Fail to prepare—prepare to fail." What does this mean? It is simple: allow time for things to go wrong. Allow, for instance, every fourth team session to be optional. That way it is still on the calendar but can be skipped if unnecessary. Plan for the robot to be ready several weeks before the actual competition, and then do meticulous testing.

While winning your competition is not the most important thing, it does feel great to have your hard work and determination recognized.

The most important thing to realize is that the robot does not need to be constructed to perform all the tasks ever imagined, and not even all the tasks required by the competition—it just needs to beat the other teams. Quite often challenges set forth at competitions end up being very demanding, and no team even comes close to accomplishing them. For example, in the nineteen years that the famous Aerial Robotics Competition (ARC) has been held, only once has a team managed to complete all the tasks required.

In practice this means that one should make a list of functionalities planned for the robot and then sort that list according to most important ones. Is it more important that the robot be fast or that it does not drop objects? Is it more important to work on its ability to recognize shapes or to enhance its body for sturdiness? Sometimes the choices are obvious, sometimes less so. Sometimes one set of functionalities depends on another, so you can't really prioritize.

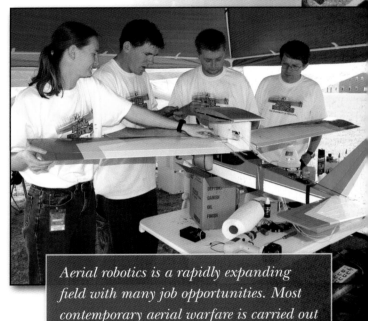

Aerial robotics is a rapidly expanding field with many job opportunities. Most contemporary aerial warfare is carried out by unmanned predator drones, i.e. robots.

Once the team is assembled and the schedule is organized, it is time to actually build the robot and get it into competition-winning shape.

CHAPTER 3
Design and Construction

The first thing to understand is that a great robot is not built—it is designed. The amount of time spent designing a robot always increases with the builder's experience. Early on it may be as low as 5 percent. Later, after many lessons learned, that percentage can go up to 90 percent or more, resulting in much more functional robots. One can safely assume that, even for a complete beginner, an hour spent designing will save at least two hours spent building, often many more.

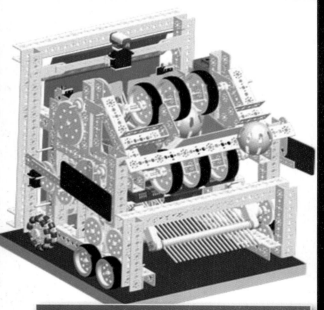

Robots can quickly become very complex, which is why design programs like CAD (computer-aided design) are necessary.

BASIC COMPONENTS

Do not reinvent the wheel when designing your robot. Yes, your team is trying to win a competition, and yes, the robot needs to be better than others. But this does not mean that the team needs to change already proven and tested concepts just to be original. If the rules must be broken, then they should be learned before being broken—more often than not there is a reason people do things in a particular way. Here are some things that should not be experimented with:

MATERIALS

Aluminum or plastics are best. Each has its advantages, and they work well together. Aluminum is light, flexible, and highly resistant to corrosion and heat. Plastics are even lighter and very sturdy and durable.

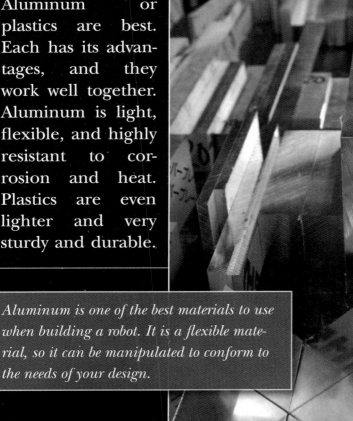

Aluminum is one of the best materials to use when building a robot. It is a flexible material, so it can be manipulated to conform to the needs of your design.

ASSEMBLY SKILLS AND SAFETY

THE SKILLS NECESSARY TO TURN DESIGN INTO REALITY ARE IMPORTANT. HOW THE ROBOT IS BUILT WILL AFFECT ITS PERFORMANCE. BUT BEFORE DOING POTENTIALLY DANGEROUS THINGS AROUND THE ROBOT, THE TEAM SHOULD BE SURE TO KNOW WHAT IT IS DOING AND HAVE PROPER ADULT SUPERVISION. DEALING WITH ELECTRICAL CURRENT CAN POTENTIALLY BE DANGEROUS. THE SAME GOES FOR ACTIVITIES SUCH AS DRILLING, WELDING, BRAZING, CUTTING, AND SOLDERING. EVEN THOUGH USING TOO MUCH OF THEM CAN BE AN INDICATION OF BAD DESIGN, THEY ARE OFTEN QUITE NECESSARY, SO IT IS IMPORTANT TO LEARN ABOUT THEM AND BECOME CONFIDENT PERFORMING THEM SOONER RATHER THAN LATER.

One would need serious reasons to use something like wood, steel, or some other nonstandard material. Almost always the robot should be kept as light as possible, and, in addition, its center of gravity kept low.

LOCOMOTION

Ninety-nine percent of the time, a simple differential drive routine will work. No need to fine-tune it. If the robot can go forward, backward, and turn, it is fine. For wheel surface, simple rubber materials that provide good friction are best. Wheel size will depend on the size of the robot, but generally the team will want to find the compromise between relatively fast locomotion and allowing enough time for the robot's sensors to detect the surroundings. For the castor low-friction plastics are best.

MOTORS AND SERVOS

Here is where the fact that a competition is in play will influence the decision process. Motors can spin freely in any direction for an unlimited amount of time. Servos have a limited range of motion, typically no more than 270°. However, servos are more sophisticated than motors, and it shows; they are much easier to control, and the sort of performance obtainable from them simply cannot be obtained from other motors. The problem with servos is that they are less intuitive and have specific voltage requirements. This translates into lower energy efficiency and potentially a bigger battery or shorter battery life, a fact that may or may not be relevant, depending on the competition.

BATTERIES

Again, this will directly depend on the type of competition being entered. Normally battery life isn't a priority because batteries can be exchanged between attempts and because robots operate for a short time to begin with. If the team goes with NiMH or NiCad, it probably won't go wrong, providing the battery fits the robot's energy needs. Alkaline batteries are not recommended. They happen to be the most common but are very low capacity and are unable to provide energy bursts in short periods. For ease of access, it is best if the robot's battery is Velcro-attached and easy to remove and replace.

MICROCONTROLLERS

Another misconception is that if one is building a cutting-edge robot, an "old" microcontroller simply won't do. Nothing could be farther from the truth. True, you won't get far with simple stamp-based controllers, but anything with decent programmability, such as Amtel's AVR, will not only do but will be capable of handling the most complicated routines sent its way. Again, it should be kept simple. A programmer (which uploads your program from the computer onto the chip) will be needed unless the team is using a microcontroller that has an inbuilt programmer, such as Cerebellum. The latter option is highly recommended for convenience.

SENSORS

Before planning for state-of-the-art sensors that will give the robot those coveted AI qualities, you should look at what is out there. Sensors usually function on a binary scale—light/dark, fast/slow—so more often than not they don't need to be sophisticated at all. A simple photoresistor can cost less than a dollar, and a pair of those can be enough to give the robot the functionality of avoiding obstacles.

SCREWS, BOLTS, AND ASSEMBLY

Keep the number of different types of screws and bolts used to a minimum. Use fewer parts, rather than more. Keep from welding and soldering as much as possible (which should be handled by an adult or professional). These are hard to undo if a mistake is made. All the heavy components of the robot should be located as close as possible to the ground—it helps stability and saves battery. In the design phase especially, the robot should be kept as "open" as possible, with parts accessible and easily removable.

A competent microcontroller is essential to a robotics competition. Because of their limited size, microcontrollers make a small-scale robot possible.

AVAILABILITY OF PARTS

The huge advantage of following the above recommendations and keeping the basic components standard is that the team will be able to find them almost anywhere. Even if no one on the team could help find them, they

Some parts of your robot you can find at your local hard-ware store or even in your own garage. For others, you may have to visit supply stores like RadioShack or even specially order online.

can be readily located online on dedicated Web sites. One can make the basics for a competition-standard robot (that can be fine-tuned and developed later on), that would include all the above components, for as low as $150, or even less; and this not by compromising on performance at all. That way you can spend time and money on parts and design decisions that really matter and really need working on.

CHAPTER 4
Building Your Robot

I n this chapter, you will learn about controlling the most important components of the robot: the servo, the microcontroller, and the robot's sensors. Also, you will find out about how to conduct smart testing that will improve the robot's performance.

MODIFYING THE SERVO

The most common reason to modify the servo is to gain speed control. The normal servo doesn't rotate continuously because of an inbuilt potentiometer ("pot") that determines the angle of the servo. Working around this problem is one of the main ways of gaining flexibility and stability.

To achieve this, you will need to open up the servo and remove the safehorn from the output shaft, to keep the gears from falling out. Also, you will want to command the servo (via the microcontroller) to rotate to 0 degrees. Then unscrew the long screws in the corners and remove the pot, located under the largest gear. After that, the servo should be centered (back to 0 degrees) and the pot head rotated until the gears stop rotating. Then the pot should be glued back into position. After that, remove the pot slot from the gear; doing so will trick the servo into thinking it remains in a constant position.

If all this is done correctly and the servo is reassembled, the robot will have achieved speed control, a very important feature for a number of tasks. Note, however, that not all robotics competitions allow for the modification of any of the motors, servos, or control systems.

THE SENSORS

Sensor understanding and control is the most important part of building a capable robot. Understanding of sensors varies considerably among enthusiasts. Most are able to use them and understand their importance but do not even begin to use their full potential. For a true competition contender, a robot needs to have more flexibility and angle control.

The key to achieving this is understanding how sensor data is interpreted in mathematical form. Data should be gathered from the sensor and put into some visualization software. Any spreadsheet software will do just fine.

Sensors allow a robot to be aware of, and interpret, the external world. Some robotics sensors are so sophisticated that they can sense objects around them.

Immediately you can find some very interesting details about how the sensor works: mistakes it makes in calculating distance, certain ranges at which it works better or worse, and many other potentially useful things. These can later be used in fine-tuning the way the sensor is controlled, correcting for its errors and achieving a very high degree of accuracy.

All this is not to say that at some point finer or more sophisticated sensors won't be necessary, but you should first make sure current ones are being used to their full potential before moving on.

THE MICROCONTROLLER

The microcontroller is the heart and soul of the robot. Having full understanding of it, what is happening inside it, and how it affects the other components and their performance is the first advanced robot construction concept that you will need to become proficient at. Knowledge of microcontroller workings will improve design, as well as the building process.

Because of this the team will probably want to become familiar with some of the more basic algorithms, such as differential drive, line following, PID control, working with timers, etc. At some point the team will also probably want to build its own microcontroller, specifically an augmented microcontroller with more than just the chip on the integrated circuit. Components can be added, like LEDs, voltage regulators, capacitors, etc.

TORTUGA II

THE BIGGEST COMPETITION FOR UNDERWATER ROBOTS IS THE ANNUAL AUTONOMOUS UNDERWATER VEHICLE COMPETITION (AUVC). IT IS SPONSORED BY THE U.S. NAVY OFFICE OF NAVAL RESEARCH. THE UNIVERSITY OF FLORIDA WON THREE TIMES IN A ROW IN THE YEARS 2005–2007. HOWEVER, THE UNIVERSITY OF MARYLAND TEAM MANAGED TO DETHRONE FLORIDA IN 2008, USING ITS *TORTUGA II* VESSEL.

THE TEAM UNDERSTOOD THE SUBTLETIES INVOLVED IN THE PARTICULAR LOCATION WHERE THE COMPETITION WAS GOING TO BE HELD, WHICH WAS SAN DIEGO, CALIFORNIA. UNDERWATER VISIBILITY CONDITIONS THERE VARY WIDELY DEPENDING ON THE TIME OF THE DAY, AND THE TEAM THUS FOCUSED MOST OF ITS EFFORT ON DESIGNING AND ADAPTING ITS SENSOR/SONAR/OPTICAL EQUIPMENT AND CONTROL SOFTWARE.

ON COMPETITION DAY, CONDITIONS INDEED PROVED TO BE CHALLENGING, AND NO TEAM HAD A STELLAR PERFORMANCE. BUT THE *TORTUGA* COLLECTED THE MOST POINTS, BEING THE BEST OF THE ROBOTS DESPITE NOT ACHIEVING ALL THE COMPETITION GOALS.

A developing board can be used, which is just a simple board with a few preexisting components that can be modified and allow very quick testing of different configurations and designs. Knowledge about controlling analog (for sensors, for example) and digital ports (for LEDs and other components) is important.

PROGRAMMING

Unless the team wants to program in machine language, which is very impractical, C is the language of choice for programming microcontrollers for robots. As stated previously, knowing what components can do and how they work together is a major part of the story, but it eventually does come down to writing the program code to control the robot's operation. The team will eventually have to have good understanding of C, which isn't

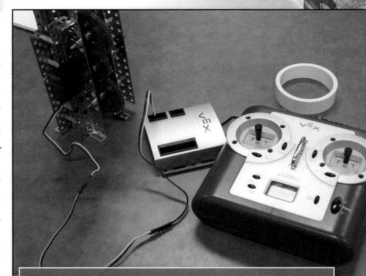

The C programming language is used in many different types of robots. This lift mechanism in this robot uses the C language to compete in the 2007 FTC game Quad Quandary.

to say that it should start writing programs from scratch; just like with components, most of the functionalities necessary have already been programmed by someone and are readily available for free somewhere online.

C has been the language of choice for a long time, but some of the more sophisticated controllers, like National Instrument's cRIO, have begun using C++. The LEGO Mindstorms NXT brick can be programmed in a specially developed version of C, known as RobotC.

For projects of any size, and especially the more complex ones, taking care of code is essential because the body of code created can quickly become too large to handle and keep track of. Fortunately there are many services that are readily available free of charge for this purpose.

TESTING

Already noted is the importance of allocating time for testing early on in the process. This becomes increasingly important as competition day approaches. There are two characteristics of good robot testing.

MODULARITY

Even the most simple robot eventually ends up being comprised of hundreds of different components. Most of these have some way of failing or otherwise not working properly. That is why it is incredibly important to test components from the early stages and to test them one by one, starting from the simplest individual ones and moving on to more complex subsystems.

This means you should test a sensor by first making sure the microcontroller is functioning well and that input/output of data is working properly. That way if the sensor is not being used, you will know for sure that the problem is a result of the sensor's malfunctioning, rather than some issue with the microcontroller or the communication channels.

In general, it is best to start testing from the individual components of the microcontroller, on to the microcontroller as a whole, and then on to other peripheral systems and components. It is amazing how often this simple principle is overlooked. The poor builders are found in a position where they simply have no way to narrow down the cause of a problem because of lack of preliminary testing.

Your robot does not need to look like a NASA project to win. A streamlined design with no unnecessary materials is the best way to fulfill most competition requirements.

REALITY

However well the robot may be working, it is important to remember that you are preparing for a competition, which means the robot will need to perform a very particular task. That is its mission and goal. Therefore to really test the robot, at the final stages of the testing schedule, the team should try out the robot on a course as close to the one in the competition as possible. Build a mock course if possible. Simulate other potential conditions, such as terrain and elements. Adhere to the timing restrictions for attempts, timing between attempts, battery recharging regulations, and any other bit of regulation that will be the rule on competition day. That way the team will be so prepared that running the competition course will feel like just another test, with great performance and no surprises.

CHAPTER 5
The Competition

When the big day arrives, if the team has been following instructions thus far and taken the time to build, fine-tune, and properly test the robot, the robot will be ready. Here are some of the details of what to expect at the competition and some inspirational examples of competition-winning robots.

Many robotics judges are former competitors themselves. Judges want to see the work in action and know exactly what they are looking for.

PREPARATION

Teams need to check in their robot, often referred to as check-in and inspections. It needs to be tested to make sure it is compliant with the competition's restrictions. This is not the time to be finding out about those restrictions, so of course the robot will have been built with the competition format, limitations, and allowed parts in mind. Some competitions do allow last-minute leeway when it comes to not-so-important parts (screws, some materials, etc.). But others are stricter, and if guidelines are not followed to the letter, the robot will be disqualified.

Meeting other contestants and the organizers is fun, but this is about winning. The team will want to examine the course and see whether it can and should make some last minute modifications on the robot. Do this only if you're sure of what is being done— there is no time for testing now. This is why the team spent all this that time testing the robot in different configurations and setups—to limit the potential for surprises.

Depending on the competition, the robot will be allowed anywhere from one to more than five runs to complete the task. Usually it is more than one—judges understand that there is a chance component involved and wish to give the best robots the opportunity to shine. Nobody wants the nightmare scenario where months of hard work are destroyed by a suddenly malfunctioning battery on the only run. Typically the best run is the one that counts, and the team should look at what is happening: how the robot is doing and how the competition is performing. Adjustments should be made, if necessary.

TEAM WILDSTANG

WILDSTANG, THE TEAM THAT WON THE 2009 FIRST ROBOTICS COMPETITION, IS A COLLABORATIVE EFFORT OF STUDENTS FROM ROLLING MEADOWS AND WHEELING HIGH SCHOOLS AND MENTORS FROM MOTOROLA IN SCHAUMBURG, ILLINOIS. THE TEAM HAS BEEN COMPETING IN ROBOTICS COMPETITION FOR MORE THAN FIFTEEN YEARS, AND THIS EXPERIENCE HAS BEEN TRANSFERRED FROM GENERATION TO GENERATION AS STUDENTS GRADUATE AND NEW ONES COME IN.

THE 2009 FIRST CHALLENGE WAS CREATED TO HONOR THE FORTIETH ANNIVERSARY OF THE MOON LANDING. IT TOOK PLACE ON A LOW-FRICTION SURFACE THAT MADE IT DIFFI-CULT FOR ROBOTS TO MANEUVER AND SERVED TO MIMIC THE LOW G CONDITIONS FOUND ON THE MOON. THE TEAM WON BY FOCUSING ON THE BASICS; IT DISCOVERED EARLY ON THAT MANEUVERABILITY, CONTROL, AND ACHIEV-ING FRICTION WERE GOING TO BE KEY TO WINNING. THE TEAM MEMBERS CON-SEQUENTLY FOCUSED MOST OF THEIR DESIGN EFFORTS ON CREATING A FOLLOWER WHEEL SYSTEM AND A SYSTEM FOR TRAC-TION CONTROL. THIS MADE

There is nothing like completing your robot, competing in your competition, and, hope-fully, winning. Since teams succeed or fail together, choosing the right teammates is key.

THEIR ROBOT'S LOCOMOTION SUPERIOR TO THAT OF OTHER CONTESTANTS.

ON COMPETITION DAY THEIR ROBOT SIMPLY OUTMANEUVERED THE OTHERS. OTHER ROBOTS HAD SUPERIOR MOON-ROCK COLLECTION ABILITIES AND MORE STREAMLINED DESIGN BUT JUST COULD NOT COMPETE WITH WILDSTANG'S CONTROL. THEY WON THE COMPETITION BY UNDERSTANDING WHAT THE CORE PROBLEM WAS GOING TO BE AND ADDRESSING IT.

LEARNING AND IMPROVING

Regardless of whether the robot wins or does not win, the team will feel that it just can't wait to go to the next competition. The excitement and the sense of fulfillment in seeing the effort result in a smart, well-running robot is hard to describe—it needs to be felt. Still, while now is definitely the time to relax and celebrate a little, you also need to look back at the entire process and reflect. Be honest. Think of things that were done right and those that could have been done better. Think of the timeline. How did the team do on following the schedule? What can be learned for the future? How did the team perform? Did it lack skills in any department? Was the mentor helpful? Were there problems finding parts, and did the robot stay within the proposed budget? All of the above need to be considered if you are to learn from the experience and make sure the next attempt at winning a robot competition is even more successful.

INTERVIEW WITH ROBOTICIST
JACOB COHEN

JACOB COHEN, A SENIOR AT BATTLEFIELD HIGH SCHOOL IN HAYMARKET, VA, WAS TEAM CAPTAIN OF THE 2010 FTC (FIRST TECH CHALLENGE) ROBOTICS TEAM 1885, WHICH CAME IN THIRD PLACE AT THE USFIRST WORLD CHAMPIONSHIP IN ATLANTA, GA. JACOB WAS A MEMBER OF ILITE (INSPIRING LEADERS IN TECHNOLOGY AND ENGINEERING) ROBOTICS, TEAM 1885, FOR THREE YEARS. DURING THAT TIME HE WORKED ON NUMEROUS ROBOTS IN BOTH FRC (FIRST ROBOTICS COMPETITION) AND FTC (FIRST TECH CHALLENGE). THROUGHOUT THOSE YEARS, ILITE ROBOTICS WON NUMEROUS AWARDS, SUCH AS ENGINEERING INSPIRATION, WINNING ALLIANCE (FIRST PLACE), AND INSPIRE, AMONG MANY OTHERS.

JACOB FIRST BECAME INTERESTED IN ROBOTICS AFTER LEARNING OF HIS SCHOOL'S TEAM. JACOB STRESSES THAT TEAMS NEED TO MARKET TO ATTRACT THE BRIGHTEST TALENT AND SAYS THAT SOME GROUPS EVEN SPREAD THE WORD VIA SOCIAL NETWORKS. OVERALL, JACOB SAYS HIS EXPERIENCE WITH ROBOTICS HAS HELPED HIM IMMENSELY, IN PARTICULAR, BECAUSE OF HIS KNOWLEDGE OF COMPUTER ENGINEERING. BY FAR, HOWEVER, THE MOST IMPORTANT SKILL HE LEARNED IS TEAMWORK, WHICH HE EXPLAINS IN THE FOLLOWING INTERVIEW.

WHAT QUALITIES DO YOU LOOK FOR WHEN CHOOSING PEOPLE FOR YOUR TEAM?

SOMETIMES YOU DO NOT GET TO PICK PEOPLE ON YOUR TEAM— YOU HAVE TO WORK WITH THE PEOPLE WHO ARE INTERESTED IN JOINING THE ROBOTICS TEAM. HOWEVER, FOR A FIRST

ROBOTICS COMPETITION, EITHER FRC OR FTC, YOU WANT A WELL-BALANCED TEAM. YOU ARE GOING TO WANT A FEW PEOPLE THAT CAN BUILD, SOME THAT CAN PROGRAM, SOME THAT CAN [WORK WITH] CAD, BUT THEN THERE ARE OTHER SKILLS THAT YOU MIGHT NOT CONSIDER.

ANY ROBOTICS EVENT THAT I HAVE PARTICIPATED IN HAS BEEN ABOUT MORE THAN JUST THE ROBOT—IT HAS BEEN ABOUT THE TEAM AND THEIR COMMUNITY OUTREACH. FOR THIS, YOU WILL NEED PEOPLE WITH GOOD COMMUNICATION SKILLS AS WELL AS GRAPHIC DESIGN SKILLS.

WHAT MAKES FOR A SUCCESSFUL TEAM?

TEAMWORK AND A HEALTHY BALANCE OF TALENTS MAKE FOR THE MOST SUCCESSFUL TEAM. ABOVE ALL OF THAT, A TEAM NEEDS A GOOD COACH [ADULT TEAM LEADER] AND MENTORS. WITHOUT THEIR GUIDANCE AND KNOWLEDGE, THE TEAM MEMBER COULD NOT RECEIVE THE KNOWLEDGE NECESSARY TO BUILD A WINNING ROBOT.

I BELIEVE THE KEY TO WINNING IS TEAMWORK, WITH BOTH YOUR TEAM AND OTHER TEAMS AT THE COMPETITION. TWO AVERAGE ROBOTS WITH TEAMS THAT CAN WORK TOGETHER WILL DO BETTER THAN TWO GOOD ROBOTS THAT CANNOT WORK TOGETHER.

WHAT CAREERS DO YOU THINK WILL OPEN UP TO PEOPLE WHO KNOW ABOUT ROBOTICS?

ANY CAREER SHOULD BE OPEN TO PEOPLE WHO HAVE PAR-TICIPATED IN ROBOTICS. ALSO, THE BIGGEST DEFICIT OF

TALENT IN THIS COUNTRY IS IN SCIENCE, TECHNOLOGY, ENGINEERING, AND MATHEMATICS (STEM). BY PARTICIPATING IN ROBOTICS, YOU STRENGTHEN YOUR TALENT IN ALL FOUR OF THOSE FIELDS.

WHAT SHOULD YOUNG PEOPLE STUDY IN SCHOOL IF THEY WANT TO GO INTO ROBOTICS?

THERE ARE NUMEROUS FIELDS INVOLVED IN ROBOTICS: DESIGNING, BUILDING, AND PROGRAMMING. ALL ENGINEERING FIELDS WILL FALL INTO SOME CATEGORY OF ROBOTICS: MECHANICAL, AEROSPACE, COMPUTER, ETC. IN ADDITION, THERE IS COMPUTER SCIENCE, THE PROGRAMMING SIDE. THERE IS A HUGE NEED FOR PROGRAMMERS IN TODAY'S WORKFORCE; I DON'T SEE THIS CHANGING ANY TIME SOON.

WHERE DO YOU SEE ROBOTICS TWENTY, FIFTY, A HUNDRED YEARS FROM NOW?

IN TWENTY YEARS, I WOULD NOT BE SURPRISED IF ROBOTS WERE WAITING TABLES IN RESTAURANTS. IN FIFTY YEARS, ROBOTS COULD BE PILOTING OUR CARS (IT'S ALREADY POSSIBLE). IN A HUNDRED YEARS, ROBOTS COULD BE FULLY INTEGRATED INTO OUR SOCIETY AS FUNCTIONAL BEINGS.

DO YOU EVER SEE ROBOTS OVERPOWERING HUMANS?

NO MATTER HOW INTELLIGENT A ROBOT GETS, IT IS STILL ARTIFICIAL INTELLIGENCE. I SEE THIS AS ALL SCIENCE

FICTION. THERE ARE NUMEROUS SAFETY MECHANISMS THAT EXIST IN ALL ROBOTS TODAY. THESE WILL ONLY IMPROVE AS ROBOTIC TECHNOLOGY IMPROVES.

WHAT ADVICE WOULD YOU GIVE A PERSON OR TEAM ON THE FIRST DAY OF BUILDING A PRIZE-WINNING ROBOT?

DO NOT EXPECT TO BUILD THE PERFECT ROBOT ON YOUR FIRST TRY. YOU'RE GOING TO HAVE TO MESS AROUND WITH MANY DIFFERENT DESIGN CONCEPTS AND PARTS UNTIL YOU FIND THE ONE THAT WORKS BEST. SO YOU'LL WANT TO SPEND SOME TIME DESIGNING WHAT YOU THINK THE BEST ROBOT IS. BUT BE CAREFUL, YOU NEED TO MAKE SURE YOU HAVE ENOUGH TIME TO BUILD AND PROGRAM THE ROBOT, AND MAKE ANY NECESSARY REPAIRS OR CHANGES.

DO YOU THINK ROBOTICS IS FOR EVERYONE?

ABSOLUTELY! IT IS BENEFICIAL TO THE TEAM TO HAVE PEOPLE WITH SPECIALIZED SKILLS IN PROGRAMMING OR BUILDING, BUT ANYONE WITH A DESIRE TO LEARN HOW TO DO THESE TASKS WILL BE FINE. SKILLS CAN BE ACQUIRED; THE ONLY SKILL REQUIRED TO BE ON A ROBOTICS TEAM IS A GOOD WORK ETHIC.

GLOSSARY

AVR A modified single chip 8-bit microcontroller developed by Amtel in 1996. This is very common in robots today because of simplicity of use and programmability.

C The C language is the most common programming language used in robotics. It is much more practical than machine code. Sometimes the more advanced C++ is used.

CAD CAD is the computer-aided design software, such as Autocad, essential for professional design of successful robots. It allows for detailed specification of processes, components, and their interaction.

capacitor The component used to store electrons (power), useful for providing energy bursts, which batteries are not capable of.

differential drive This is the simplest locomotion mechanism. It is for going forward. Both wheels turn at the same speed, and for going backward, it is the same but in the opposite direction. Turning is achieved by one wheel turning in one direction and the other in the other direction.

expected forces Forces expected to be applied on particular parts of the robot (joints, components) during the robot's operation, and especially during some high-stress tasks.

LED Light-emitting diode.

line following An algorithm that makes a robot's movement dependent on a predesignated line.

microcontroller A chip used to receive feedback and send instructions to a robot's components. Usually it is augmented with other components apart from the chip, such as LEDs, resistors, etc.

modularity A testing methodology that focuses on testing individual components first, moving on to larger subsystems, and eventually the entire robot. It is essential for error detection, especially on more sophisticated projects.

pathfinding The act of discovering a route, or the best/quickest route between two positions. It is one of the most important features of a robot. Commonly existing algorithms are used. Strong reasons are necessary for customizing these algorithms.

photoresistor A type of resistor whose resistance decreases with increasing light density.

PID controller Stands for proportional integral derivative controller. It denotes any controller that has an inbuilt control loop feedback mechanism. It is useful in designing a robot's control mechanism and easy to directly program through custom or already available algorithms.

pot Short for potentiometer, a pot is part of a servo motor. It is connected to the output and serves to vary power input; also called variable resistor.

power requirements This refers to both voltage and power requirements of the robot and its individual components.

servo A type of motor that has built-in gearing and feedback correction for greater control.

voltage regulator A component commonly found on an augmented microcontroller. It is used to control voltage input, most commonly to keep it stable.

FOR MORE INFORMATION

MIT Artificial Intelligence Laboratory
545 Technology Square
Cambridge, MA 02139
Web site: http://www.ai.mit.edu/projects/
    humanoid-robotics-group
This extremely cutting-edge, research-oriented group is
    at the Massachusetts Institute of Technology.

The Robotics Institute
Carnegie Mellon University
5000 Forbes Avenue
Pittsburgh, PA 15213-3890
Web site: http://www.ri.cmu.edu
The most serious nongovernmental robotics institute
    on the East Coast, the Robotics Institute provides a
    wealth of information on a variety of topics related to
    automation and robotics.

Robotics Society of Southern California
800 N. State College Boulevard
Fullerton, CA 92831-3547
Web site: http://www.rssc.org
The RSSC organizes its own competition each year and
    is one of the biggest societies by membership in the
    United States.

Seattle Robotics Society
P.O. Box 1714
Duvall, WA 98019-1714
Web site: http://www.seattlerobotics.org

The Seattle Robotics Society has plentiful information on its up-to-date Web site about building advanced robots and attending competitions.

Vancouver Robotics Club
Room SW3-2745
British Columbia Institute of Technology
3700 Willingdon Avenue
Burnaby, BC V5G 3H2
Canada
Web site: http://vancouverroboticsclub.org
This very active club at the British Columbia Institute of Technology is entirely dedicated to preparing its members for robotics competitions.

Western Canadian Robotics Society
1301-16th Avenue NW
Calgary, AB T2M 0L4
Canada
Web site: http://www.robotgames.net
This is Canada's most active robotics society and the organizer of RoboGames.

WEB SITES

Due to the changing nature of Internet links, Rosen Publishing has developed an online list of Web sites related to the subject of this book. This site is updated regularly. Please use this link to access the list:

http://www.rosenlinks.com/robo/pwr

FOR FURTHER READING

Branwyn, Gareth. *Absolute Beginner's Guide to Building Robots.* Indianapolis, IN: Que Publications, 2004.

Bridgman, Roger Francis. *Robot.* New York, NY: DK Publications, 2004.

Brown, Jordan. *Robo World: The Story of Robot Designer Cynthia Breaze.* New York, NY: Franklin Watts, 2005.

Chapman, Sarah. *The Robot Book.* Hauppauge, NY: Barron's Educational Series, 2006.

Cook, David. *Robot Building for Beginners.* Berkeley, CA: Apress, 2004.

Gifford, Clive. *Robots.* Boston, MA: Kingfisher, 2003.

Jefferis, David. *Robot Voyagers.* New York, NY: Crabtree Publishing Company, 2007.

Jefferis, David. *Robot Workers.* New York, NY: Crabtree Publishing Company, 2007.

Piddock, Charles, and J. D. Lee. *Future Tech: From Personal Robots to Motorized Monocycles.* Washington, DC: National Geographic, 2009.

Siciliano, Bruno, ed., and Oussama Khatib. *Springer Handbook of Robotics.* Berlin, Germany: Springer, 2008.

Singer, P. W. *Wired for War: The Robotics Revolution and Conflict in the Twenty-First Century.* New York, NY: Penguin Press, 2009.

White, Steve. *Military Robots.* New York, NY: Children's Press, 2007.

Yes magazine editors. *Robots: From Everyday to Out of This World.* Toronto, CA: Kids Can Press, 2008.

BIBLIOGRAPHY

Appin Knowledge Solutions. *Robotics.* Hingham, MA: Infinity Science Press, 2007.

Choset, Howie M. *Principles of Robot Motion: Theory, Algorithms, and Implementation.* Cambridge, MA: MIT Press, 2005.

Huang, Han-Way. *PIC Microcontroller: An Introduction to Software and Hardware Interfacing.* Clifton Park, NY: Thomson/Delmar Learning, 2005.

Jazar, Reza N. *Theory of Applied Robotics: Kinematics, Dynamics, and Control.* New York, NY: Springer, 2007.

Mataric, Maja J. *The Robotics Primer.* Cambridge, MA: MIT Press, 2007.

Perdue, David J. *The Unofficial LEGO Mindstorms Nxt Inventor's Guide.* San Francisco, CA: No Starch Press, 2008.

Platt, Charles. *MAKE: Electronics: Learning by Discovery.* Sebastopol, CA: O'Reilly, 2009.

Predko, Michael. *123 Robotics Experiments for the Evil Genius.* New York, NY: McGraw-Hill, 2004.

Siciliano, Bruno. *Robotics: Modeling, Planning and Control.* London, UK: Springer, 2009.

Siegwart, Roland, and Illah Reza Nourbakhsh. *Introduction to Autonomous Mobile Robots.* Cambridge, MA: MIT Press, 2004.

Spong, Mark W., Seth Hutchinson, and M. Vidyasagar. *Robot Modeling and Control.* Hoboken, NJ: John Wiley & Sons, 2006.

Thrun, Sebastian, Wolfram Burgard, and Dieter Fox. *Probalistic Robotics.* Cambridge, MA: MIT Press, 2005.

INDEX

ABOUT THE AUTHOR

Joel Chaffee is a writer of nonfiction and fiction, and is currently at Columbia University. His academic career includes studies in history, literature, cinema/filmmaking, and writing. A wonder at the natural world caused him to further pursue knowledge in the fields of science and mathematics, and even robots.

PHOTO CREDITS

Cover, p. 9 Jens Schlueter/AFP/Getty Images; back cover and interior © Axel Lauerer/Flickr/Getty Images; pp. 4, 35 Adriana M. Groisman, courtesy of FIRST; p. 8 Steve Van Meter, VideoRay LLC; pp. 13, 16, 31, 33 Chelle Hambric, ILITE Robotics; p. 14 Meg Guckenberg, ILITE Robotics; p. 17 © AP Images; p. 18 Tyler Hambric, ILITE Robotics; p. 19 Bloomberg via Getty Images; pp. 23, 26 Shutterstock.com; p.24 Hill Street Studios/Blend Images/Getty Images; p. 29 Jacob Cohen, ILITE Robotics.

Designer: Matthew Cauli; Editor: Nicholas Croce; Photo Researcher: Peter Tomlinson